ORCHII

GLENROTHES

ELIZABETH CORDINER

WINDFALL BOOKS

EDITED BY LILLIAN KING

ISBN NO:978 955278 3 9

Acknowledgement

Dedicated with love and gratitude to Jill Bennett, WEA and her writers' group, Glenrothes.

A catalogue record for this book is available from the British Library

The FIFE NEW POETS series is funded by Fife Fringe

Printed by A4 Print Dunfermline
Cover design by Belle Hammond
Art work by Jim Douglas
Typesetting, layout and design by Windfall Books
Published by Windfall Books, Kelty
01383 831076
windfallbooks@tiscali.co.uk
wwww.windfallbooks.co.uk

ELIZABETH CORDINER

Elizabeth, a retired Headteacher, was born in Denbeath and educated at Denbeath Primary and Buckhaven High School before training as a teacher in colleges in Dundee and Edinburgh. She lives in Glenrothes.

Her short stories have been published by D.C Thomson Ltd and she won the Fife Libraries 2006 short story competition. Her first published poem was in her High School's glossy magazine. Elizabeth loves writing, playing with words, drinking coffee, music, humour, dancing and completing The Scotsman crossword. Her favourite word is gorgeous.

CONTENTS

orchids in Glenrothes

green-stemmed, pink-lipped
orchids in Glenrothes,
a flash of varnished toes
in the shopping Centre,
a rainbow over the Post Office.
God saying 'Hiya.'

Bonded

I'm in a library.
For the first time,
with my dad
I'm very young.
I have a ticket.

In a warm room
full of light,
there is a table,
with books, all sizes,
some open, showing coloured illustrations.

I'm choosing one of these marvels,
to take home with me,
hug, smell, turn its pages,
lose myself inside its world.

With my dad now in another room.
darker,
with narrow racks
labelled with letters, signs.
It's grown-up reading.

He chooses.
Westerns first, Zane Grey,
then Crime.

Edgar Wallace and 'The Four Just Men,'
Neil Gunn, the 'Para Handy' tales,
he piles them up.

I wait, respectful of the rites,
wide-eyed, discovering,
but recognising, claiming this for me
as quiet readers move
with a shared purpose,
in between the shelves.

Going home
we're on the motor bike,
doubly bonded now,
first by blood and bone,
and now for ever
by the love of words.
And that is how we stayed throughout our lives,
sometimes at peace together,
sometimes at war,
but always fellow-travellers.

He introduced me to this other world
so early in my life
that it has been a part of who I am.
For this most precious gift,
I thank you, Dad.

Memories

We would be throwing things,
apple cores and bits of orange peel,
throwing them at the screen, and sometimes at each other,
as the baddie in the black hat sneered and snarled,
and we would yell and hiss at him:
and when the pigmies in the jungle made a circle round the hero,
threatening him with their spears,
necklaces made from teeth around their necks,
I'd take my sister's hand and clasp it tight,
holding my breath until they let him go,
or worshipped him,
falling onto their knees,
mesmerised by a mirror or a convenient eclipse.

I see them still,
the cowboys in the pristine shirts, the masked avenger,
figures from the children's matinees.
We'd give our pocket money to be there,
gripped by the images,
enthusiastic, cheering in the worn plush seats.
Life was so vivid on the screen, exciting,
served in weekly episodes, where everything was sorted,
goodies were triumphant,
and the hero got the girl.
We would go home contented, satisfied,
not knowing that a happy ending would not always come,
no matter how we wished,
and that in later life
we could not trust a hero would be riding into town
to sort our messy grown-up lives for us.

The cage

I tried to stretch my wings.
I told him I was leaving
many times.
Each time,
the cage,
his cage,
repossessed me.
He visited.
He had a life outside
the cage,
but I had none.
Sometimes
I'd see the sky,
the mountains,
feel for a moment
the unfolding of feathers,
the power in flight,
and I would tell him
once again,
No more.
Now,
I know
that I am here
till one of us should die.
I cannot go through the door
of the cage
though
it is always
open.

Five flower poems

I never met a flower I didn't like
or a lily I couldn't take to
or a stand-offish hyacinth.
I get on with them all,
always have.
treat them as you would like to be treated, I say.

besides, they're lovely.

If I met a flower for a coffee,
I'd say,
how are your petals today?
then we'd chat about our lives,
the flower and I.
Same time next week?
I'd say,
but the flower wouldn't commit.

might be dead by then.

I'd gladly buy a meal for a flower,
or a ticket for a show,
give my phone number,
say you're looking great,
and mean it.

If only a blind date
was more like a flower

my bonsai tree flowered.
it's true.
tiny white blooms of jasmine.
then today,
an orange appeared.
I kid you not,
an orange.
it's like an arboreal magician.

next week,
the flags of all nations.

When I opened the door,
a hyacinth stood there in the rain.
soaked it was,
the water streaming from its pink blossom.
oh, come in,
I said,
out of the rain.
there's always a cup of tea here.
we sat till midnight,
the hyacinth and I,

then we both went
to our beds.

I saw you

time stood still
when I saw you
birds stopped in mid-flight
wings unfurled
secret soft feathers shown
a petal from a flower suspended
in its fall
all was silent
waiting
then the key turned
in the clockwork Cinderella
and she danced in circles
the earth lurched
then settled
birds flew again
the petal dropped
but nothing ever after was the same
colours scents tastes
the feel of things was different
after
I saw you

Thick lensed

thick-lensed,
heavy,
plastic-rimmed,
with imitation crystals set into the frames,
smudged and spotted,
worn,
one of the legs bent,
discarded now,
of no more use,
sitting on the night table
beside the body on the bed,
once fashionable,
once admired,
seen in a hundred photographs,
in Blackpool
for the Lights,
under a wide-brimmed hat
at Elsie's wedding,
picked up each day
and taken off each night,
no more,
my mother's glasses.

The nun's story

I sit with folded hands.
The chair is old and hard.
There is no comfort there.
Bones, wood, and the harsh cloth that covers me,
we make another trinity.

'Pray for us sinners now, and at the hour of our departing.'

I sew for the little black children.
My fingers are raw.
The needle stabs into the linen,
and draws blood,
dripping onto my skirt, red on the black.
It seems profane.
I thought there was no blood in me.
I am colourless.

'Holy Mary, Mother of God.'

There is nothing about me that is soft,
nothing rounded, nothing easy.
I am all angles.
My joints ache,
my hands are claws,
my feet twisted in the high black shoes,
the nails bruised and black.

Last night I dreamt
that I was running
easily through the grass,
long-haired again.

‘Forgive me, Father, for I have sinned.’

I hate this place, the candlesticks,
the scent of polish on the floor,
the creaking of the door when the sisters file through,
Bernadette’s coughing in the night,
Father Bryan’s breath.

‘Mea culpa, mea culpa, mea maxima culpa.’

I walk with pain to my room.
I feel the rosary swing
against my hip.
I take off my cap,
undo my belt, and in my shift,
I wash.
I kneel before I sleep.

‘Pray for us now.’

Tonight I will be free again,
ride with the horses
as I used to do
before I wore Christ’s ring.

You remind me of a man

An hour before school -
I'm reading the bottle on the table.
It's breakfast time, and I need to read something.
'Cette sauce célèbre de haute qualité
est un melange d'épices orientaux.'
'Cette sauce célèbre,' I say to John.
'Eh?' says my younger brother.
'It's on the sauce bottle,' I mumble.
'I can speak French too,' John says.
'Bon jour, fair midden.'
I laugh.
'You've been watching Francie and Josie.'
He laughs, too, pretends to swagger.
He's now a Glesga ned on the pull.
We go into the patter together.
'Hullawrerr, china.'
'Ur ye dancin'?' says John.
'Ur ye askin?' I say.
'Ah'm askin,' says John.
'Then ah'm dancing.'
John and I memorise patter like some people memorise
poems.
We're away now, leaning over the table, engrossed.
'You remind me of a man,' says John.
This is an old favourite.
We take a line each.
'What man?' I say.
'A man with a power.'
'What power?'
'The power of voodoo.'

'Voodoo?'
'You do.'
'You do what ?'
John finishes triumphantly -
'You remind me of a man.'
Neither of us can remember what film that comes from.
Mum shouts through from the little kitchen,
and John heads upstairs to the bathroom.
I finish my roll.
I dream, my eyes unfocused, my legs warm
from the coal fire,
until I hear Dad coming in from his milk round,
bringing with him the cold morning air.
It's time to join the real world.
I find my bag.
As I cycle to school, on the bike that's too big for me,
I remember it's double French this afternoon,
with Mr. Clark.
Wonder if Clarkey likes H.P. sauce?

What was it that kept me there?

What was it that kept me there
when you cried every night,
or when you ran away and told me that you hated me?
What was it that kept me there
when you stopped coming home,
and when they found you, broken, in an alley?
What was it that kept me there
when I fed you when you could not feed yourself,
lifted up your head to drip the water through your lips,
while you stared unseeing past my shoulder?
What was it that kept me there
when you could feel life's hurts no more?
Foolish, forgiving, bloody, magnificent love.

The thief

My neighbour's peas,
hanging below slender corkscrew curls,
firm padded pods, warm from the sun,
a sharp green in the nose,
and with the green, the scent of earth
and furry busy caterpillars;
Stretching to reach fat peapods,
I hold them smooth on my palm,
and longer than my little hand.
I tear the thin raised strings along their edges,
snapping,
to see inside
the smooth globes, all neatly packed in rows,
babies in baskets.
Then, sweetness, clarity, a burst of flavour,
tongue wet with juice,
hot hands stained,
and empty pods lying,
evidence,
upon the summer grass;
nothing else,
ever,
like the taste
of stolen peas

The catch

He stopped the engine, and the boat rocked gently.
The northern sky was empty, and there was no wind,
the sky, the sea, the island, suddenly unreal,
a painted picture he had chanced to enter.
How strange it was he should be there,
with lobsters safely in the creels,
and whisky waiting for him on the shore.
He had turned the boat around, away from harbour,
following an instinct, a strong pull,
a need,
like the desire for water when you were dry,
or to see a face that was gone for ever.
So he had struck out into the blue, and now he waited, simply waited.
For what, he did not know.
After a while, he did not think at all.
And then the sea began to move, forming circles,
and, smacking the water,
came a long, greeny-blue tail.
He bent over, peering into the sea,
and when the head came up, he was as close to it as his own hand.
The head was followed by a body, woman's breasts and belly,
two long arms that rested on the boat's side.
Her skin was nacre, mother-of-pearl.
It had a bluish sheen.

It shimmered.
The planes of her face were perfect,
carvings on a cameo shell.
Her hair was long, thick, colourless,
like a seaplant, strands twined together, floating gently in the water.
He had never seen a face like hers.
It was the sea's face, her eyes blue-white pools,
and yet he saw within them, breaking waves.
She reached out with long, webbed fingers,
and when they touched his skin, he shivered with their cold.
She pulled him down into the sea,
and he went slowly, as in an accident,
or in a dream.
She drew him down, deeper still.
He was himself no more, for he was hers,
with no desire but for
the mermaid.

Rid

See me
Ah'm mad, me
Ah'm rid
Ah shout ma name
Ah'll no' be overlookit
Or mistooken
No' me
Ah'm in your face
Ah'm rid
No' like that icy-lippit blue
Or sappy broon
Ah've goat attitude
Ah'm up for it
Ah'm hoat
Move ower'n let the talent through
Ah'm rid!

Morning view

Light
through my window,
the sky flushed with rose.
I rise,
head full of dreams.
Peace
hangs over the toytown below.
I watch,
bare feet tapping to music from the radio,
as the town wakes up.
Cars begin to move,
the ecstatic sky clouds
and dulls.
The morning soils,
becomes another day,
grubby with our doings
and our beings.
Yet
it will come again,
baby-new,
so we can try again
to make the day
as filled with promise
as the
perfect
morning.

Meals on wheels

Come in, hen.
Aye, I ken ye've loats o' denners tae deliver,
bit a wee bit sate'll help ye, wull it no'?
Sit doon beside me. Mak' an auld man happy.
There.
Ye're lookin' weel. I've no seen you fur ages. It's been
yon wee crabbit flamer wi' the ginger perm that's broat ma
meal.
Oh, that's yer sister? Sorry, hen.
An' hoo am ah?
Ah'm jiggered, pal.
Ah'm knackered,
sittin' in the same auld chair, an' lookin' through they same
auld windaes-
twa pun' fifty fur tae hae them cleaned? It's daylight
roabbery-
an' a' fur whit?
The same auld rotten view, jist broken gless an' dog shite.
Aye, ah swear they're breedin' they Alsatians.
Every day they're sniffin' roond ma door.
Ah ken whit ah wid dae,
ah'd shoot the lot o' them,
bang bang, then nae bark bark.
Huh - better no' tae laugh. Ma chest's sair.

Whit---- ye're gaun' awa' areadies?
Ach, ye've shairly goat five meenits oot yer day.
Aw weel then, dinnae bang the door.
Ah dae ken, they're a' the same;
a'body's rushin'- an' fur whit?
When ah wis young, there wis a reason, an' a purpose, an' a
pint tae everythin'.
Noo there's jist gettin' throo the days, an' listenin' tae the
tick o' that b… cloack-
ah telt them no tae bother when ah left the work, bit naebody
listens onymair.

‘Fur forty years o’ keepin’ time’,
an’ that’s a laugh, fur why in God’s name wid ah want time
tae be kept
noo that ma Jeannie’s gone?

Whaur hae ah gone?
Whaur is the laddie playin’ Kick the Can ,
wha kept a pile o’ coamics an’ a torch, tae read at nicht.
Whaur is the teddy boy wi’ velvet collar and duck’s erse,
that used tae get a lumber oan a Setterday?
Nane o’ that “Are ye dancin’” shite;
ah wis a richt wee patter merchant, so ah wis.
Ah coud fair pu’ the burds, an’ tak them up a close an a’.
Noo look at me,
auld men’s slippers an’ a shaky haund,
fit for the coup.
Aw weel, at least ah’ve goat ma smokes,
an’ mince an’ tatties in ma tin, if ah’m no’ wrang (it’s
Wednesday the day).
Come oan, ye auld fule, pit the kettle oan, an’ hae a fag.
It coud be worse.
It coud be macaroni cheese.

Life's Playground

Things didn't go the way they should have.
It's my ball and I want it back.

Nobody gave me what I needed.
It's my ball and I want it back.

They've all got more than me.
I never got the breaks.
Not playing anymore.
It's my ball and I want it back.

You chose somebody else.
I'm telling mum on you.

You left me on my own.
I'm telling mum on you.

No-one looks after me.
I do it all myself.
You're going to pay for this.
I'm telling mum.

I didn't mean to.
It's not my fault.
A big boy made me do it. It was him.

I wasn't there.
It isn't fair.
A big boy made me do it. It was him.

It was an accident. It wasn't me.
I never touched it. It just tore.
A big boy made me do it. It was him,

and I'll never never do it any more.

I did not realise

I did not realise that they would end,
that suddenly, or so it seemed,
the old streets and the places would be gone,
left only in the mind, yet still so clear.
When did they go?
While I was occupied with other things
that did not matter.

I did not realise that they would end,
my times with Dad and Val
and Phil and Anne, who'd call me on the telephone,
yet whom I never took the time to meet,
although I promised see you soon.
And one by one they went,
while I was busy with my life.
I did not realise how much it mattered
but I do now.
Now that they've gone.

Ah huv so goat wan

Ah huv so goat wan, so ah huv
You're no' tae say ah'm a leear
Ah huv so goat an alligator in the bath
an' ah'm its boss
It dis whit ah say
or it disnae get its denner
Whit dis it like but?
It likes big boys like you, ha ha

Ah huv so goat wan, so ah huv
You're no' tae say ah'm a leear
Ah huv so goat a python under the bed
an' ah'm its boss
It dis whit ah say
Whit dis it dae but?
It crushes big boys like you, ha ha

Ah huv so goat wan, so ah huv
You're no' tae say ah'm a leear
Ah huv so goat an albatross on the roof
an ah'm its boss
It dis whit ah say
Whit dis it dae but?
It poos on big boys like you, ha ha

Ah huv so goat wan, so ah huv
You're no' tae say ah'm a leear
Ah huv so goat a tiger in the press
an' ah'm its boss
It dis whit ah say
Whit dis it dae but?
It waits till it's dark
then it comes oot
an' it goes doon the stairs
an' oot the door
an' doon the steps
an' alang the road
till it comes tae the hoose
that you live in, ha ha

Ah huv so goat wan, so ah huv
You're no tae say ah'm a leear
Ah huv so goat
an imagination, ha ha.

freedom

we had camped by the sea,
that's when we first saw them,
in the distance
the first small clouds of dust.
as they drew nearer,
chariots appeared,
the horses staring-eyed,
the riders helmeted.
they had pursued us.

we cried out in fear,
has God abandoned us,
His chosen ones?
have all our years of suffering been for this?

some spat at Heaven,
rent their garments in despair,
others, like me,
knelt down and prayed,
the prayers that are a part of who we are,
that Father Abraham had prayed
in time of need.
He heard our prayer.

Moses raised up his arm across the sea
it fell apart
as if a mighty wind had blown.
we ran,
the towering waters right and left of us,
holding our children as we ran
we cried to one another,
sobbing and looking back
for still they came.

their wheels spun,
but they followed in their hundreds
through the path that He had made appear.
horsemen were thrown from squealing mounts,
yet they came on,
we fleeing still before them.

when the last of us were safe
he stretched his arm again.

at daybreak, it began.

the waters rushed back, thundering, till there was no division,
hit them,
tossed and lifted them,
screaming,
from their chariots,
broke their chests.
the sea was filled with blood.
not one survived.

day after day I saw the bodies,
Egypt's pride,
knocking against each other,
hair spread out like seaweed,
bloated arms
with bangles
glittering in the sun,
and then the horses,
oh God, all the horses,
Pharaoh's best,
bellies blown,
burst carcasses,
drifting.

I found a whip
washed up upon the sand,
engraved and dedicated to some heathen god.
I have it still. I don't know why.

closing my eyes today,
I see them,
covering the waters,
faces upturned
with sightless eyes,
mouths open in eternal scream.
so many dead.
my woman sleeps beside me in the dark,
outside the tent a dog howls,
soon it will be light
and we must leave again.

but I will take them with me,
all the dead,
into the Promised Land.
I am a prisoner still.
they shackle me,
enslave me with their silent cries.
I never will be free of them.

Faither's chair

Faither had the big chair,
the one beside the fire.
No-one else sat there,
only Faither.
There he read his paper,
had his cup of tea, two sugars.
Faither's children knew that,
always, faithers got the best.
Faither had respect from us,
obedience.
That was his right because
he worked for us
and also just because
he was the faither.

And that is what he stayed
until the day he died.
He was the faither,
and the chair was always
Faither's chair.

Old and Young

I was never older than when I was young,
bowed down by adults' worries,
unable to control events,
pinned, stuck, helpless.

Now I laugh like a baby,
am happy in my own skin,
freed.
As I get older I get younger.
What a turnaround.